THE PSYCHOLOGIST'S TEST FILE

An Illustrated Handbook of Sample Test Items

THE PSYCHOLOGIST'S TEST FILE

An Illustrated Handbook of Sample Test Items

Patricia W. Clemens, MA

Academic Therapy Publications
Novato, California

Academic Therapy Publications
20 Commercial Boulevard
Novato, California 94947-6191

International Standard Book Number: 0-87879-355-0

2 1 0 9 8 7 6 5 4 3
0 9 8 7 6 5 4 3 2 1

CONTENTS

Introduction 7
Auditory Discrimination 13
Auditory Memory 17
Concentration 21
Conceptual Thinking 27
Environmental Intelligence 33
Expressive Language 37
Numerical Reasoning 43
Reading 55
Reasoning 59
Receptive Language 65
Spelling 69
Visual Discrimination 71
Visual Memory 79
Visual-Motor Coordination 85
Index 91

INTRODUCTION

It is now usual for one-fifth to one-fourth of a school population to have been given individual assessment batteries consisting of an IQ test, achievement tests, and probably some other kinds of tests. This has come about as a result of Public Law 94-142, which requires that each child be educated according to his ability to learn. As part of estimating a child'a ability to learn, a professional other than the child's regular teacher, usually a psychologist, tests the child individually. It is hoped that these tests will help provide an unbiased picture of the child's strengths and weaknesses.

Despite their frequent use, the tests in the individual assessment batteries are poorly understood by classroom teachers and parents alike. Both what the tests measure and the statistical interpretation of their results may be misunderstood.

Parents sometimes refuse to allow their children to be tested because they do not understand what psychoeducational testing is. Reasons parents have given, or reluctantly admitted to, for refusing permission to test have included:

- Fear that the tests might in some way harm their child.
- Certainty that their child was not "crazy," and an assumption that only those suspected of being "crazy" would be asked to take such tests.
- Fear that the child might reveal family secrets while being tested.

When parents refuse to permit testing, it often means the child will not be given the materials and individualized instruction he needs to improve his ability to achieve in school.

Because access to the content of standardized tests is limited to those who are qualified to give them, many teachers do not have a clear picture of the kinds of tasks the child can do well and the kinds of tasks the child has difficulty doing, as indicated by test results. This makes it very awkward for teachers to discuss test results with parents in concrete terms and makes it difficult for them to help plan the child's educational program. Even those who are qualified to give these tests may have trouble explaining the student's performance, because they are restricted from revealing the content of test items.

In short, psychoeducational tests need to be explained to a large number of people, both before and after children are tested. The teacher must be able to discuss test results with parents and use test results in helping to plan the child's educational program. Yet the actual content of the tests must not be revealed if the tests are to remain valid and reliable.

Introduction

The purpose of this handbook is to provide a concise reference for understanding the content of popular psychoeducational tests without revealing actual test items. Examples and visual aids offer the best means of making tests intelligible. Therefore, this handbook provides a brief explanation of test scores and many examples of test items similar to those found in current, popular tests. The facsimile test items are grouped into sections according to the abilities they assess.

Handbook Users and Uses

This handbook is an effective reference for those who must explain test results and for those who must understand where a student failed in order to turn test results into instructional goals and objectives. Possible users and uses of this handbook include:

Teachers and Psychologists

- To help parents or guardians give informed consent for testing.
- To dispell fear of psychological testing on the part of either the one to be tested or the one giving consent.
- To determine what kinds of test items were given in an assessment. Such information is helpful in determining whether the individual was actually tested in the area of observed disability or proficiency. It is also helpful in deciding what additional testing is needed.
- To help in explaining test results by showing how test scores are determined and by providing examples of the kinds of tasks the child was asked to carry out.
- To provide concrete examples of the child's strengths and weaknesses for the purpose of educational planning.

College Instructors

- To give students in education and psychology an idea of the variety of ways in which abilities are assessed.

About Testing

To get an indication of how well an individual understands and copes with his world, the examiner will frequently test a number of abilities, using a variety of standardized tests. It is rare for an individual to perform equally well in all areas sampled. Usually, there is a pattern of strengths and weaknesses that can be identified by understanding what each task measures. Small differences between test scores, or a single score out of line with the rest of the scores, should not be considered proof of a strength or weakness unless they are confirmed by other formal or informal measures.

The examiner does his best to make the person being tested feel confident about being tested. At the beginning of a new task, help is frequently given. It might be a demonstration of what is wanted, a sample problem to work, feedback as to the correctness of a response, or an opportunity to try again. Tasks that are beyond the test-taker's ability are quickly abandoned. The examiner maintains an encouraging, non-judgmental attitude throughout the testing.

About Test Scores

When the abilities of many people of similar age are tested, their scores fall into a pattern that can be shown by the drawing on page 9. The drawing is called the "normal curve." The high part of the curve shows where scores of more people in a population fall. These scores are average, neither very high nor very low. The low parts of the curve, at the left and right, show the numbers of people getting very low and very high scores. In testing abilities on standardized tests, there are always a few who get these extreme scores.

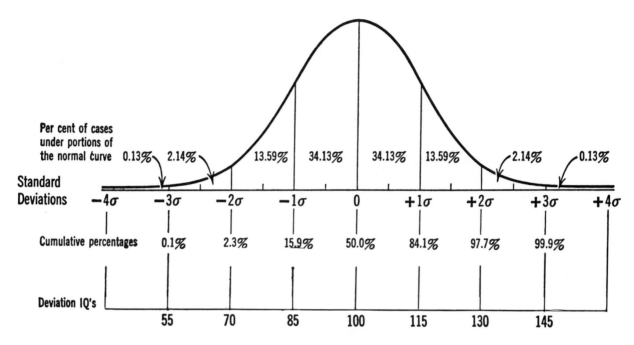

Per cent of cases under portions of the normal curve 0.13% 2.14% 13.59% 34.13% 34.13% 13.59% 2.14% 0.13%

Standard Deviations -4σ -3σ -2σ -1σ 0 $+1\sigma$ $+2\sigma$ $+3\sigma$ $+4\sigma$

Cumulative percentages 0.1% 2.3% 15.9% 50.0% 84.1% 97.7% 99.9%

Deviation IQ's 55 70 85 100 115 130 145

The normal curve has the same shape as one that would be made by taking all the test forms from a large population and stacking at the left end of a shelf all the forms with low scores and making a new stack to the right for each successively higher score. Deviation IQ scores and percentile rankings are ways of stating how an individual performs in relation to others of his age and nationality, that is, *where* his score falls on that shelf.

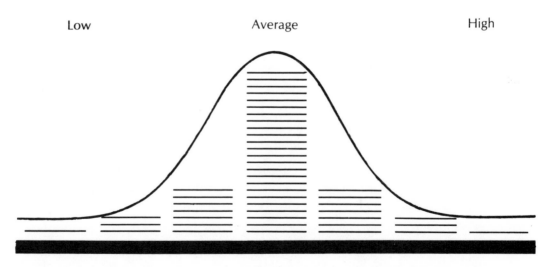

Low Average High

Grade and age scores are meant to be indicators of the school grade or age of children who performed at the level when the test was standardized. A number of factors need to be kept in mind when considering grade scores.

- The scores are frequently based upon the number of correct responses the child makes, not *which* responses were correct. If a child were given a page of mathematical problems and he missed or skipped some early easy problems yet responded correctly to problems in algebra, trigonometry, and calculus, his grade score would not reflect his true ability.

- Not all children begin school at the same age or progress through school at the same rate.
- Not all schools teach the same skills in the same grade.

In the same way, age scores should be viewed with some skepticism. The four-year-old who attains an age score of four years has a much different pattern of skills than a fifteen-year-old who attains the same score of four years. Scores that are based on the normal curve, though not perfect, are much better indicators of where a child stands in relation to his peers than are either grade or age scores.

Organization of the Handbook

This handbook is organized into sections based on the ability being tested by the facsimile test items. For example, all of the tasks that measure the individual's ability to remember what he hears are described in the section titled Auditory Memory; all tasks that are heavily dependent on the test-taker's ability to focus and maintain attention are described in the section titled Concentration. If a particular task is a good measure of more than one ability, it will be described in more than one section. An exception to this rule is that the tasks described under Expressive Language are not also described under Receptive Language, even though the tasks may tap similar underlying skills. Also, items modeled on achievement tests are not described in more than one section. It must be kept in mind that no test item can be said to measure just one ability. All the tasks described in this book require the ability to focus attention, understand some form of language, and remember the instructions long enough to carry them out.

Fourteen sections that identify the classification of test items are included. Within each section, facsimile test items are numbered. The Test-Subtest Index, which lists widely-used tests, identifies sample test items by the section abbreviation and item number. Each of the sections is described below and its abbreviation, as used in the Index, is presented.

Auditory Discrimination (AD) is the ability to hear and tell the difference between sounds. This ability is essential to the use of phonics in reading and spelling.

Auditory Memory (AM) is not only the ability to remember what is heard, but also to repeat it in some way or act upon it. The child may be asked to recall something he has just heard or to recall something he heard repeatedly in the past. Examples of this skill in everyday life include dialing a telephone number the operator has just given, playing "Simon Says," and remembering the lyrics and tune of a popular song.

Concentration (C) is the ability to focus on one thing while not being distracted by either the internal or external environment. Everyday examples are the ability to read or study in the midst of noise and chaos, and the ability to continue to play football without being aware of an injury.

Conceptual Thinking (CT) is the ability to see relationships between things and ideas. It allows us to see the relationships between a nail and a staple, a sphere and a cube, love and hate, and poverty and affluence.

Environmental Intelligence (EI) is the ability to remember, interpret, and use the information presented in daily life. Examples of this include dressing appropriately for the weather, knowing when holidays come, and behaving appropriately in a given situation.

Expressive Language (EL) is the ability to understand and use words appropriately. It is seen in young children when they demand more to eat and in presidents when they explain that what they are proposing is not new taxes, but the closing of tax loopholes.

Numerical Reasoning (NR) is the ability to reason using symbols to determine and express relationships between things and ideas. Examples in everyday life include determining how toys should be divided between two children, doubling a recipe, and designing efficient aerodynamic shapes.

Reading (Rdg) is the ability to gain meaningful information from written words and, in the context of this handbook, to be able to identify letters of the alphabet and use phonics to pronounce written words or nonsense syllables.

Reasoning (R) is the ability to use information to solve problems, understand the past, and prepare for the future.

Receptive Language (RL) is the ability to understand language without necessarily being able to speak, write, or sign it. This is seen in pre-verbal children when they are asked if they want a bottle and in people who, through injury, have lost the ability to use language expressively, though they continue to understand language. Receptive language is both the language we speak and write, and the language we do not actively use but understand when we hear or read it.

Spelling (S) is the ability to indicate the order in which letters should be placed to make a recognizable word. In the context of this book, it is also the ability to discriminate between, and to name, letters of the alphabet.

Visual Discrimination (VD) is the ability to see the difference and similarities between objects. In everyday life this skill is used in selecting fruit that is ripe, but not overripe, matching socks, reading, and in drawing and painting.

Visual Memory (VM) is the ability to remember what has just been seen, seen some time ago, or has been seen repeatedly in the environment. This ability is used in reading, writing, matching patterns from memory, and remembering friends and acquaintances.

Visual-Motor Coordination (VMC) in this context, is the ability to coordinate eye and hand movements. In everyday life this skill is used in activities such as picking up blocks, threading a needle, and working on an assembly line.

How to Use This Handbook

This handbook may be used in two ways: 1) section headings, listed alphabetically in the Contents, may be used to guide you to items that test specific abilities and 2) the Test-Subtest Index may be used to guide you to facsimile items for a particular test or subtest.

If you are interested in devising tests that might give an indication of students' visual memory skills, ideas can be found in the section titled Visual Memory. If a student is suspected of having poor ability to reason abstractly, the section on Conceptual Thinking might provide ideas for tasks that can be used in giving him practice in this area.

The Test-Subtest Index lists, in alphabetical order, the tests upon which the facsimile test items are based. If you need an indication of the kinds of tasks a child was given on a particular test, you can look up the test in this index. For example, if you want to know the types of tasks required of a child on the *Stanford-Binet,* levels IV through VI, you can find the *Stanford-Binet* listed alphabetically in the Index and the year-levels in order after that heading. For each subtest in the year-level there will be one or more references to a section and item number. Because many test items are good measures of more than one ability, the same facsimile item may be presented in more than one section.

As an example of using the Index, under *Stanford-Binet,* level IV, subtest 6, you will find the same facsimile tasks in the sections on Expressive Language (item 9), Reasoning (item 4), and Environmental Intelligence (item 5). Often, as in this case, facsimile items are given for a range of ability levels. It will be left to the judgment of the user to select the appropriate item(s). If for example, you look in the Index under *Wide Range Achievement Test,* Arithmetic subtest, the Index will refer you to 21 different facsimile items in the handbook. In addition to each of these items being different, they also represent a range of ability levels, just as the tasks on the subtest do.

The facsimile test items included in this handbook are representative of those that appear in a wide range of psychoeducational tests. Although the test items have been keyed only to those tests identified as the most widely used, the items are similar in format to those that appear on many other tests. When a particular test is not listed in the Index, representative items can generally be found by determining the section that corresponds to the area of assessment and inspecting the facsimiles within that section.

AUDITORY DISCRIMINATION

Auditory discrimination

Tasks such as the following are used to measure how well the test-taker discriminates between similar sounds.

1. The test-taker is shown a page with a number of pictures on it. The pictures illustrate words that are very similar in sound. A word is presented clearly and without background noise. The test-taker is then asked to select the picture that best shows the word. Words and pictures such as the following are used:

carry

raining

travel

2. The test-taker is shown a page with a number of pictures on it. The pictures illustrate words that are very similar in sound. A word is presented clearly but with background noise. The test-taker is then asked to select the picture that best shows the word. The level of the background noise gradually increases as the test progresses. Words and pictures similar to those given in the example above are used.

3. The examiner reads pairs of words, some of which are identical and some of which are slightly different. He then asks the test-taker to say whether the two words were the same or different. Words such as the following are used:

> raging-paging
> hazed-fazed
> blazer-blazer
> based-paced
> heart-hurt
> mammal-mammal
> telling-tilling

4. The examiner reads pairs of words, some of which are identical and some of which are slightly different. He then asks the test-taker to repeat the words he has just heard. Words such as those listed above are used.

AUDITORY MEMORY

AUDITORY MEMORY

Tasks such as the following are used to measure how well an individual remembers what he hears.

1. The examiner slowly says a series of numbers, or other non-meaningful sounds, and the person is asked to repeat them. If the test-taker is successful at repeating the series, he may be asked to repeat a longer series. Series such as the following might be used:

<table>
<tr><td>5-3</td><td>1-4</td></tr>
<tr><td>2-4-1</td><td>6-3-2</td></tr>
<tr><td>7-5-6-2</td><td>8-9-7-5</td></tr>
</table>

2. The examiner slowly says a series of numbers and the test-taker is asked to repeat them backwards. If he is successful at repeating the series, a longer series may be given. Series such as those listed above might be used.

3. The examiner says a word normally in all ways except that one or more sounds is omitted. The test-taker is then asked to say the complete word. Words such as the following are used:

SPA / ETTI spagetti THUN / ER thunder
· SKATE / OARD skateboard / OAL / INER coal miner
/ ACE SHI / space ship

4. The examiner says the component sounds of words or nonsense syllables with distinct breaks between sounds. The test-taker is then asked to say the word in the usual way. Words and letter combinations such as the following are used:

m-ilk   s-n-a-ke   a-p-$\bar{u}$-g-$\bar{o}$ b-$\bar{i}$-d-$\bar{e}$-n

5. The examiner slowly says a group of unrelated words and then asks the test-taker to repeat them. The number of words in the group is gradually increased. Groups of words such as the following are used:

book-hat-tree knob-paint-foot-wheel-dust
mouse-flag-glasses dog-nail-iron-sheet-head
air-hand-light-egg cloud-pencil-dot-idea-fun-art
stick-ball-paper-purse ear-mat-table-poem-rain-diet

6. The examiner asks the test-taker to perform a task, or tasks, in a certain order. Tasks such as the following are given:

> Put this ruler on the desk.
>
> Put this eraser beside the tablet, move the chair up to the table, then bring me the ruler.

7. The examiner says sentences of increasing length and asks the test-taker to repeat them. Sentences such as the following are used:

> The helicopter took off.
>
> Water vapor condenses to form clouds.
>
> The mountains were half hidden by the drifting mist.
>
> Martha was not hurt when her motorcycle skidded on the gravel, but her head-light was broken.

8. A page of designs set in rows is placed before the test-taker. The examiner then gives the test-taker a series of increasingly complex instructions as to how he is to mark the designs with a pencil. Designs such as the following are used:

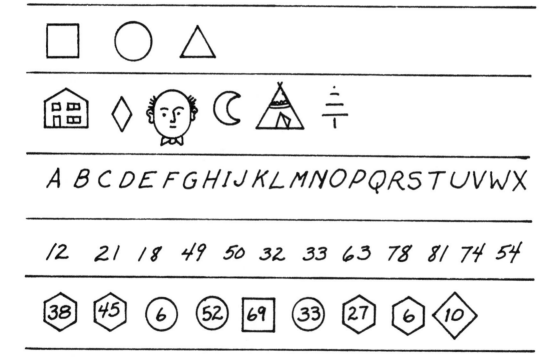

Instructions such as the following are given orally then marking begins:

> Put a circle in the triangle and a line in the box.
>
> Draw a ring around the moon, a line over the house, and a dot under the tree.
>
> Draw a line under S, a line over M, and a line through J.
>
> Put circles around the number that is in the twenties, the number that is one less that 8 X 8, the number that is 6 X 2, the number that is 10 X 5, and the last number in line.
>
> Put lines under the 6 in a hexagon, the odd number in a circle, the biggest number in a hexagon, and the odd number in the hexagon nearest 10.

9. The examiner gives the test-taker a printed copy of a story. He then tells the test-taker to listen carefully while the story is read, because questions will be asked about it. After reading the story aloud, the examiner removes the printed copy and questions the test-taker about it. A story similar to the following is used:

In The Dark

Mark and Jeff were afraid of the monster who lived in their closet. His name was Hairy Man. He only came out of the closet when it was very dark. Mark and Jeff always left a little light on in their room. One night there was a big storm. All the lights went out. Mark and Jeff thought they saw Hairy Man at the foot of Jeff's bed. Just then the lights came back on. They saw that the monster was really Jeff's bathrobe on the bedpost. After that, Hairy Man always stayed in the closet, even when it was very dark.

Questions such as the following are asked:

What was the name of this story?

Who was afraid?

What was in the closet?

What happened?

10. The examiner reads a short passage to the test-taker, explaining beforehand that he will be expected to remember the main thoughts of the passage. A passage such as this one from *On Liberty*, by John Stuart Mill, is read, and the test-taker is asked to relate its main thoughts.

A person may cause evil to others not only by his actions but by his inaction, and in either case he is justly accountable to them for the injury. The latter case, it is true, requires a much more cautious exercise of compulsion than the former. To make anyone answerable for doing evil is, comparatively speaking, the exception.

CONCENTRATION

CONCENTRATION

Tasks such as the following are given to measure how well an individual can direct and confine his attention to an assigned task.

1. The examiner asks the test-taker to perform a task, or tasks, in a certain order. Tasks such as the following are given:

    Put this ruler on the desk.

    Put this eraser beside the tablet, move the chair up to the table, then bring me the ruler.

2. The examiner places a pile of tiles with various designs on the testing surface. Then, after putting just the tiles needed for the task before the test-taker, the examiner briefly displays a card showing the sequence into which the decorated tiles are to be placed. The test-taker is then given two chances to copy the sequence from memory. Design sequences such as the following are used:

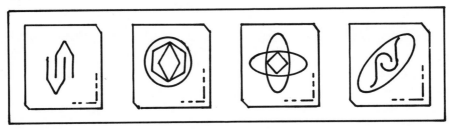

3. The examiner slowly says a series of numbers, or other meaningful sounds, and the person is asked to repeat them. If the test-taker is successful at repeating the series, he may be asked to repeat a longer series. Series such as the following might be used:

5-3	1-4
2-4-1	6-3-2
7-5-6-2	8-9-7-5

4. The examiner slowly says a series of numbers and the test-taker is asked to repeat them backwards. If he is successful in repeating the series, a longer series may be given. Series such as those listed in the preceeding task might be used.

5 . After the examiner briefly shows the test-taker a card that presents a sequence of pictures of common objects, the test-taker is asked to list the pictures from memory. The number of pictures on each card is very gradually increased. Cards showing pictures such as the following are used:

6 . The test-taker is given part of a design. He is briefly shown the completed design and then asked to complete the design he was given from memory. Incomplete and complete designs such as the following are used:

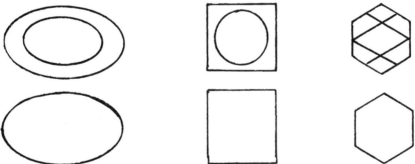

7 . The test-taker is shown one or more designs briefly and then asked to draw the design or designs from memory. Designs such as the following are used:

Concentration

8. The examiner says sentences of increasing length and asks the test-taker to repeat them after him. Sentences such as the following are used:

> The helicopter took off.
> Water vapor condenses to form clouds.
> The mountains were half hidden by the drifting mist.
> Martha was not hurt when her motorcycle skidded on the gravel, but her headlight was broken.

9. The examiner briefly shows the test-taker cards with letters on them and then asks him to list the letters from memory. The number of letters to be remembered is gradually increased. Letter series such as the following are presented:

BH   GIF   NDQR   MLOZB   CXHJKP

10. The examiner presents the test-taker with a picture that has been divided into equal pieces and the pieces scrambled. The test-taker is then asked to map how the parts of the picture should be placed to make a logical picture. The scrambled parts are numbered. These numbers are used to indicate on the "map" where each piece goes. The puzzles are similar to these:

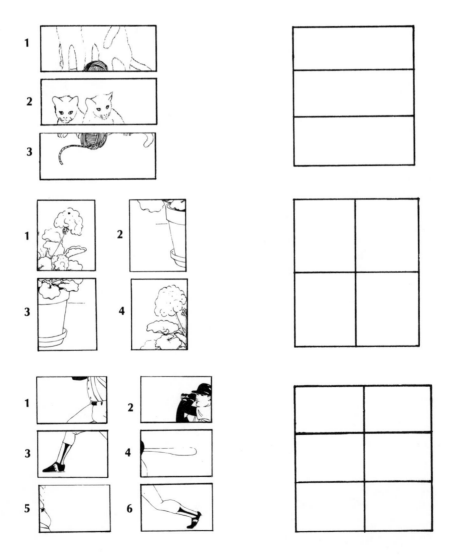

1 1 . A page of designs set in rows is placed before the test-taker. The examiner then gives the test-taker a series of increasingly complex instructions as to how he is to mark the designs with a pencil. Designs such as the following are used:

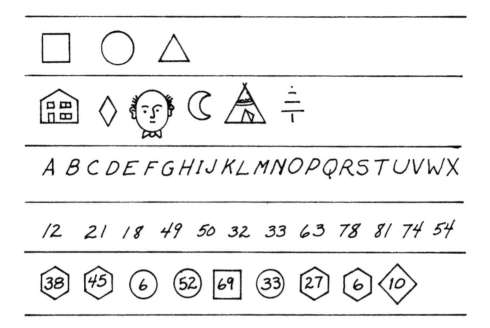

Marking begins after each set of oral instructions is given. Instructions such as the following are given:

Put a circle in the triangle and a line in the box.

Put a ring around the moon, a line over the house, and a dot under the tree.

Put circles around the number that is in the twenties, the number that is one less than 8 X 8, the number that is 6 X 2, the number that is 10 X 5, and the last number in line.

Put lines under the 6 in a hexagon, the odd number in a circle, the biggest number in a hexagon, and the odd number in the hexagon nearest ten.

12. The examiner gives the test-taker a printed copy of a story. He then tells the test-taker to listen carefully while the story is read, because questions will be asked about it. After reading the story aloud, the examiner removes the printed copy and questions the test-taker about it. A story and questions similar to the following are used:

In The Dark

Mark and Jeff were afraid of the monster who lived in their closet. His name was Hairy Man. He only came out of the closet when it was very dark. Mark and Jeff always left a little light on in their room. One night there was a big storm. All the lights went out. Mark and Jeff thought they saw Hairy Man at the foot of Jeff's bed. Just then the lights came back on. They saw that the monster was really Jeff's bathrobe on the bedpost. After that, Hairy Man always stayed in the closet, even when it was very dark.

Questions such as the following are asked:

What was the name of this story?

Who was afraid?

What was in the closet?

What happened?

13. While the test-taker watches, the examiner strings beads in a certain order and tells the ex-
     aminee he will be asked to string beads in the same order. After letting him look at the bead
     pattern for a short time, the model is put away and the test-taker is asked to duplicate it from
     memory. Designs such as the following are used:

14. The examiner reads a short passage to the test-taker, explaining beforehand that he will be ex-
     pected to remember the main thoughts of the passage. A passage, such as this one from *On
     Liberty*, by John Stuart Mill, is read and the test-taker is asked to relate its main thoughts in his
     own words.

     A person may cause evil to others not only by his actions but by his inaction, and in
     either case he is justly accountable to them for the injury. The latter case, it is true,
     requires a much more cautious exercise of compulsion than the former. To make
     anyone answerable for doing evil is, comparatively speaking, the exception.

15. Using a key, the test-taker must enter appropriate symbols into the corresponding design. He
     is encouraged to work as quickly as he can. Tasks such as the following are given:

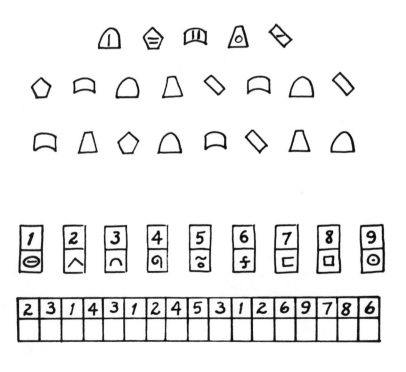

16. The test-taker is asked to work orally presented arithmetic problems in his head. The prob-
     lems can be presented only once and the test-taker is so forewarned.

CONCEPTUAL THINKING

CONCEPTUAL THINKING

Tasks such as the following are used to measure an individual's ability to work with abstract concepts.

1. The test-taker is shown a picture of an item. Then, from pictures of a variety of items, he is asked to find another one of the same kind. Pictures such as the following are used:

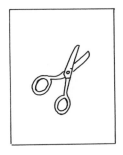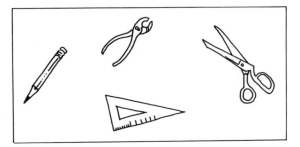

2. The examiner asks the person being tested to complete statements such as:

   A rock is hard: a pillow is _____.

   A frog hops: a snake _____.

   Cardboard is stiff: paper is _____.

   Remarks off the subject are inane: remarks on the subject are _____.

3. The examiner points to the center picture and asks, "What goes best with this?"

4. The examiner points to the top left picture in the grid of four and then to the bottom left picture and says, "If this goes with this, then which of these six pictures should go with this picture (pointing to the one next to the top left)?"

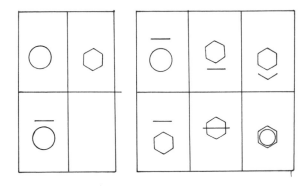

5. The examinee is shown three or more drawings, or designs, and asked to tell which one of the group does not belong.

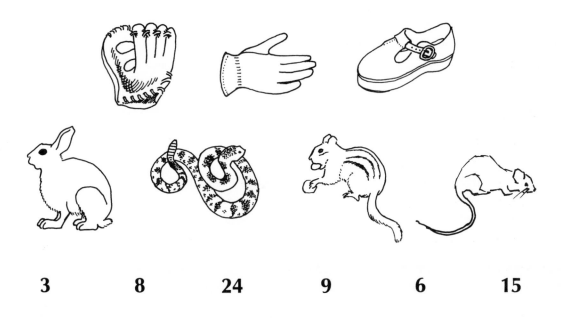

3   8   24   9   6   15

Conceptual Thinking

6. The test-taker is shown a picture and then is asked to indicate which of a number of other pictures shows the opposite of the first picture.

	A	B	C

7. The examiner says a word and then asks the test-taker to say a word that means just the opposite. Words such as the following are used:

fat	multiply	conform	ubiquitous
easy	divorce	candor	erudite
narrow	elevate	polemic	procrastinate

8. The examiner asks the test-taker questions such as:

Which is larger, a cup or a coffee pot?

Which is older, a mother cat or her kitten?

9. The test-taker is asked to tell in what way items such as the following are alike:

a. carrot-lettuce
b. dog-horse
c. radio-television
d. gun-fishing rod
e. monaural-binaural
f. apogee-perigee
g. good-bad
h. friend-enemy
i. malignant-benign
j. pleasure-misery
k. fear-horror
l. industrious-productive

10. The examiner presents pairs of words and asks the test-taker to tell in what way the items are different. Pairs of words such as those listed in the preceeding example are used.

11. The examiner presents trios of words and asks the test-taker to tell in what way the items are alike. Words such as the following are presented:

     red-green-blue   ballet-concerto-play

     pan-skillet-casserole   statue-painting-drawing

12. The examiner recites a saying then asks the test-taker to tell what it means. Sayings such as the following are used:

     All's well that ends well.

     It's not whether you win or lose, but how you play the game.

     Beauty is in the eye of the beholder.

13. The test-taker is shown a pattern with a missing section, or sections, and is asked to indicate what should be used to complete the pattern. Designs such as the following are used.

14. The test-taker is asked to read and complete analogies such as:

     monthly is to *weekly* as *daily* is to _____.

     cattle is to *calves* as *goats* is to _____.

     ecstatic is to *joyous* as *despondent* is to _____.

Environmental Intelligence

ENVIRONMENTAL INTELLIGENCE

Tasks such as the following are used to measure the individual's alertness to, and ability to cope with, the environment.

1. After being shown a picture of an object, the test-taker is instructed to demonstrate (mime) appropriate actions for using it. Common items, such as a pencil, needle and thread, and bicycle, are pictured.

2. The examiner shows the test-taker a picture and then asks him to tell what is not right, or is silly, about that picture. Pictures such as these are used:

3. The examiner asks the test-taker to tell what is not right, or is foolish, in statements such as these:

    Ellen used the bucket with no bottom in it to carry water from the well.

    My mother's wife is handsome, though he is bald.

    Because I am an only child, my brothers and sisters tease me.

4. The examiner asks the test-taker to solve practical problems requiring the use of common sense. The problems are similar to the following:

    What is the thing to do when you get a headache?

    What is the thing to do if the milk you are drinking, or the food you are eating, tastes spoiled?

    What is the thing to do if you are playing a game and the other person cheats you?

5. The examiner asks the test-taker about familiar events, customs, and attitudes such as:

    What do we do with our noses?

    Why do people have cars or trucks?

    Why should a person learn to read?

    Why is it important for the labels on food to list what is in the food?

    Why do we have to pay taxes on many of the things we buy?

    In what ways are large cars better than small cars?

    What are the advantages of having a president of the United States?

6. The examiner asks the test-taker to respond to items such as:

    Which is larger, a cup or a coffee pot?

    Which is older, a mother cat or her kitten?

    Put your left hand above your right hand.

    Show me my left leg.

    If today is Thursday, what day was the day before yesterday?

    How can you figure which years are leap years?

7. The test-taker is shown a picture of a social situation and asked to tell about it. Pictures such as the ones shown below are used to stimulate responses:

8. The test taker is asked what various objects are made of. Questions such as the following are asked:

    What is a car made of?

    What is a cup made of?

    What is a toothbrush made of?

9. The test-taker is asked to name calendar sequences. Frequently a check is made of the test-taker's understanding of the sequence, if his initial response was correct, by asking a question such as, "What season came before spring?"

10. The examiner describes a situation to the test-taker and then asks him to name the event or explain what is happening. Descriptions and questions such as the following are given:

   A man got out of a car that had a red, white, and blue poster taped to each side. He then went to each house on the street, spoke enthusiastically to each person that came to the door, usually shook each person's hand, and always gave each person a small card. What do you think the man was doing?

11. The test-taker is asked questions about his environment, such as:

   In what way are lettuce and celery alike?

   In what way are a spoon and a cup alike?

   In what way are a can opener and a brass bowl alike?

   In what way are honesty and thoroughness alike?

12. The individual being tested is asked to arrange pictures such as these to tell a logical story:

EXPRESSIVE LANGUAGE

EXPRESSIVE LANGUAGE

Tasks such as the following are used to measure how well an individual expresses himself verbally (usually orally).

1. The examiner asks the person to complete statements such as:

    A rock is hard: a pillow is _____.

    A frog hops: a snake _____.

    Cardboard is stiff: paper is _____.

    Remarks off the subject are inane: remarks on the subject are _____.

2. The examiner gives the test-taker an object, such as an eraser, and says, "Tell me all about this." The examiner then counts the number of appropriate responses that are given within a certain time limit.

3. While showing an appropriate picture, the examiner asks the person being tested to complete statements such as:

    a. Here is a candle. Here are two _____.

    b. Here is a goose. Here are two _____.

    c. A, B, and C are the first, second, and _____ letters of the alphabet.

    d. I gave you the last book. I can't give you _____.

4. The examiner says a word normally in all ways except that one or more sounds is omitted. The test-taker is then asked to say the complete word. Words such as the following are used:

    SPA / ETTI spagetti   THUN / ER thunder
    SKATE / OARD skateboard   / OAL / INER coal miner
    / ACE SHI / space ship

5. The examiner shows the test-taker a picture and then asks him to tell what is not right, or is silly, about that picture. Pictures such as these are used:

6. The examiner asks the test-taker to tell what is not right, or is foolish, in statements such as these:

    Ellen used the bucket with no bottom in it to carry water from the well.

    My mother's wife is handsome, though he is bald.

    Because I am an only child, my brothers and sisters tease me.

    Jim played the title role in the class play, *The Tempest*.

7. The examiner says a word and then asks the test-taker to say a word that means just the opposite. Words such as the following are used:

fat	multiply	conform	ubiquitous
easy	divorce	candor	erudite
narrow	elevate	polemic	procrastinate

8. The examiner asks the test-taker to solve practical problems requiring the use of common sense. The problems are similar to the following:

    What is the thing to do when you get a headache?

    What is the thing to do if the milk you are drinking, or the food you are eating, tastes spoiled?

    What is the thing to do if you are playing a game and the other person cheats you?

9. The examiner asks the test-taker about familiar events, customs, and attitudes such as:

    What do we do with our noses?

    Why do people have cars or trucks?

    Why should people learn to read?

    Why is it important for the labels of food to list what is in the food?

    Why do we have to pay taxes on many of the things we buy?

    In what ways are large cars better than small cars?

    What are the advantages of having a president of the United States?

10. The examiner asks the person to say as many words as he can think of, giving as examples words such as: room, light, bug.

11. The examiner presents pairs of words and asks the test-taker to tell in what way the items are alike. Pairs of words such as the following are presented:

a. carrot-lettuce   g. good-bad
b. dog-horse   h. friend-enemy
c. radio-television   i. malignant-benign
d. gun-fishing rod   j. pleasure-misery
e. monaural-binaural   k. fear-horror
f. apogee-perigee   l. industrious-productive

12. The examiner presents pairs of words and asks the test-taker to tell in what way the items are different. Pairs of words such as those listed in the preceeding example are used.

13. The test-taker is shown pictures of various objects and asked to name them. Pictures such as the following are shown:

14. During the testing session, the examiner notes the test-taker's ability to use word combinations and sentences spontaneously.

15. The examiner asks the test-taker to name a variety of familiar objects. Toy representations of objects such as the following are used to draw out these responses: flower, pan, chicken, bicycle.

16. The test-taker is shown a picture of a social situation and asked to tell about it. Pictures, such as those shown below, are used to elicit these responses.

17. The test-taker is asked what various objects are made of. Questions such as the following are asked:

> What is a car made of?
>
> What is a cup made of?
>
> What is a toothbrush made of?

18. The test-taker is asked to give the meaning of various words such as these:

a. pillow	g. connect	m. sorrow
b. wagon	h. miracle	n. patriotism
c. coat	i. sample	o. challenge
d. storm	j. digest	p. republic
e. criminal	k. weevil	q. oblivious
f. medium	l. happy	r. pervasive

19. After explaining what a rhyme is, the examiner asks the person being tested to either think of as many words as he can to rhyme with a given word, such as "bold" or "drew," or think of a specific word to rhyme with a given word. Tasks such as the following might be given:

> Tell me the name of a piece of furniture that rhymes with red.
>
> Tell me the name of part of the body that rhymes with wreck.

20. The examiner presents trios of words and asks the test-taker to tell in what way the items are alike. Words such as the following are presented:

> red-green-blue
>
> pan-skillet-casserole
>
> ballet-concerto-play
>
> statue-painting-drawing

21. The examiner presents sentences with an essential word, or words, missing and asks the test-taker to complete it. The task may be either written or oral. Sentences such as the following are presented:

> When we got to the lake we had a picnic _____ then went fishing.
>
> She is feeling much better _____ she got the medicine she needed.
>
> The space shuttle is expensive _____ not _____ expensive _____ building a new ship for each trip.

22. The examiner gives the test-taker a card on which are printed scrambled sentences. The test-taker is then asked to unscramble the sentences. Sentences such as the following are presented:

> quickly home he toward walked
>
> man up chair old got his the slowly from
>
> compete the of flag children the for honor the raising

23. The examiner recites a saying and then asks the test-taker to tell what it means. Sayings such as the following are used:

> All's well that ends well.
>
> It's not whether you win or lose, but how you play the game.
>
> Beauty is in the eye of the beholder.

24. The test-taker is asked to make up sentences using words provided by the examiner. Groups of words such as the following are given:

    murky, submerge, intention

    eloquent, feeble, petition

    affable, mendacious, confound

25. The test-taker is asked questions about his environment, such as:

    a. What do you call this? (Point to your nose.)

    b. How many arms do you have?

    c. From what animal do we get wool?

    d. Name the largest river in the United States.

    e. What two chemical elements combine to make water?

    f. How many things make a gross?

    g. What is the main material used to make steel?

    h. What is the capitol of Canada?

    i. How far is it from New York to Chicago?

    j. Who was Charles Dickens?

    k. Where is New Zealand?

NUMERICAL REASONING

NUMERICAL REASONING

Tasks such as the following are used to measure how well an individual works with mathematical concepts.

1. The test-taker is asked to say which of two piles of small objects, or which of two objects, is the larger, smaller, longer, et cetera.

2. The test-taker is asked to count various quantities of objects.

3. The test-taker is asked to count by a variety of units.

4. The test-taker is asked to work orally-presented basic arithmetic problems in his head, such as:

    a. $5 + 1 = $ _____. $3 + 9 = $ _____. $6 + 7 - 2 = $ _____.

    $5 + 7 + 8 \div 4 = $ _____. $6 \times 5 + 6 \div 9 - 4 = $ _____.

    b. Fred had three kites. One got caught in a tree. How many kites did Fred have left?

    Mrs. Smith bought twelve tomato plants at three plants for a dollar. How much change did she get back from a ten-dollar bill?

5. The test-taker is asked to identify numerals.

6. The test-taker is asked to say which of a pair of numbers is the greater.

7. A page of designs set in rows is placed before the test-taker. The examiner then gives him a series of increasingly complex oral instructions as to how the designs are to be marked. Designs such as the following are used:

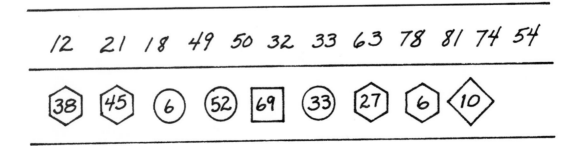

Instructions such as the following are given:

Put circles around the number that is in the twenties, the number that is one less than 8 X 8, the number that is 6 X 2, the number that is 10 X 5, and the last number in line.

Put lines under the 6 in a hexagon, the odd number in a circle, the biggest number in a hexagon, and the odd number in the hexagon nearest 10.

8. The test-taker is asked to give, or show, the examiner various quantities of small objects, such as beans.

9. Given pictures of solid geometrical forms, such as a stack of blocks, the test-taker is asked to infer information about them. For example, given pictures such as those below, the examiner might ask how many blocks, or how many sides, the shape has, counting both the seen and the unseen sides.

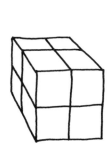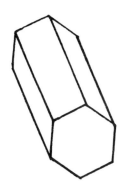

10. While the test-taker watches, the examiner folds a piece of paper through the middle. He then unfolds it and asks him to say how many compartments it is divided into. The paper is then folded again on the original fold and then at right angles to the first fold through the middle. The test-taker is asked to guess how many compartments the paper will be divided into. His guess is either confirmed or denied by unfolding the paper. This procedure is continued until the examinee can predict how many compartments there will be with each successive fold and give the rule for predicting the number, or until a set number of folds has been made.

11. The test-taker is asked to solve problems (which may be repeatedly presented at his request) such as these:

On a camping trip a father sent his daughter, Mia, to a spring to get exactly 3 cups of water. He gave her a 5 cup jar and a 2 cup jar. How could Mia bring back exactly 3 cups of water? Begin by filling the 5 cup jar.

Mia was then sent to get rice from a large bag. She was given an 8 cup jar and a 5 cup jar and asked to bring back exactly 7 cups of rice. How could Mia do it? Begin by filling the 5 cup jar.

12. The test-taker is given or shown cards on which are printed arithmetical word problems. He is asked to read each problem aloud, or to read along as it is read to him, and then solve it in his head. He may reread the problem at will. Problems such as the following are presented:

If 3 pieces of candy cost 10 cents, what will be the cost of 12 pieces?

An artist earns $500 for each picture he paints. The cost of his materials is $20. He works 40 hours on each picture. How much does he earn per hour?

13. The test-taker is asked to solve problems such as the following in his head.

> A medicine man taught two boys how to make magical potions. These two each taught two others. How many knew how to make magical potions altogether, including the medicine man?

> In the fifth grade the teacher taught 5 students to knit, and each of these taught 5 more. Altogether, how many people in the fifth grade knew how to knit?

> The first issue of a newspaper sold 200 copies, the second issue sold 300, and the third issue sold 450. If sales continue to increase at this rate, how many copies of the fourth issue will be sold?

14. The test-taker is asked to supply the missing number in sequences such as these:

$$2 \quad \underline{\hspace{1cm}} \quad 6 \quad 8 \quad 10$$
$$1 \quad 7 \quad \underline{\hspace{1cm}} \quad 19 \quad 25$$

15. The test-taker is shown a pattern with a missing section, or sections, and is asked to indicate what should be used to complete the pattern. Designs such as the following are used:

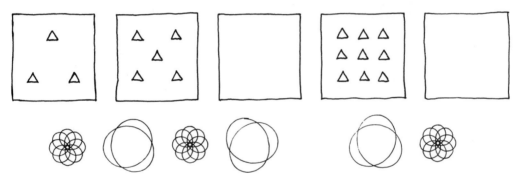

16. The test-taker is asked to count certain objects in a picture. For example, he might be asked to tell how many stars are in a picture such as this:

17. Given a certain number, such as 11, the test-taker is asked to tell what number comes before and/or after it.

18. The examiner counts a few objects using ordinal numbers and then asks the test-taker to say the next ordinal number.

19. The test-taker is shown a picture of various quantities of objects and then is asked to tell the difference in the quantity of the largest and smallest groups. Pictures such as the following are used:

The test-taker might be asked to answer a question such as:

The smallest group has how many fewer things than the largest group?

20. The test-taker is asked to identify quantities written in Roman numerals.

21. The test-taker is asked to tell how many of one number there is in another, such as, "How many 15's are in 63?"

22. The test-taker is asked to tell why one number is smaller than another number, or numbers, using numbers such as:

36.7　　　　　69　　　　　9.25　　　　　9/12　　　　　8/10

23. The test-taker is asked to round numbers to the nearest tenth, hundredth, thousandth, and so on, and then read them.

24. The test-taker is shown a number, or numbers, written with an exponent and asked to tell the value of the number(s).

25. The test-taker is asked to tell the relationship (ratio) of one number to another. Numbers such as the following are used:

6 : 30　　　　　　　7 : 56　　　　　　　6 : 72

26. The test-taker is asked to respond to questions involving basic understanding of fractions, such as:

a. If half of these balloons burst, how many would be left?

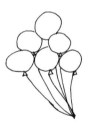

b. Half of this square is white. How much is striped?

c. Read this numeral for me. 2/5

d. Two-thirds of these hats is how many?

e. Read this fraction as a mixed number. 13/3

f. Write this fraction as a percent. 6/9

27. The test-taker is asked to give the name or meaning of various mathematical shapes, symbols, and abbreviations. Tasks such as the following are given:

Point to the circle (rectangle, oval, hexagon).

Explain what these symbols mean. + − × =

What do these abbreviations mean? ft. lb. yd. hr. mm.

28. The test-taker is shown an illustration of a geometric configuration, given information about it, and then asked to make a deduction. Given are tasks such as:

What can you tell me about these two triangles if angle A is equal to angle D, angle B is equal to angle E, and side AB is equal to side DE?

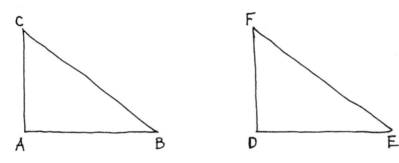

29. The test-taker is asked to work addition problems such as these:

a. If two rabbits are in the garden and another one joins them, how many are there all together?

b. Given a pencil and a sheet on which are printed problems such as these, the test-taker is asked to work as many as he can.

		389		
2	82	54	2/3	6 1/2
+5	+4	+106	+1/3	+3 3/8

30. The test-taker is asked to work subtraction problems such as these:

    a. If you have six ribbons and give four away, how many are left?

    b. Given a pencil and a sheet on which are printed problems such as these, the test-taker is asked to solve as many as he can.

$$\begin{array}{ccccccc} 6 & 13 & 45 & 407 & 58.4 & 3/5 & 7\ 1/8 \\ -2 & -7 & -14 & -92 & -6.8 & -1/3 & -4\ 3/4 \end{array}$$

31. Given a pencil and a sheet on which are printed multiplication problems such as these, the test-taker is asked to solve as many as he can.

$$\begin{array}{cccc} 4 & 7 & 16 & 4.30 \\ \times 1 & \times 3 & \times 5 & \times 29 \end{array} \qquad 6\ 1/3 \times 7 = \underline{\hspace{1cm}}$$

32. The test-taker is asked to work division problems such as these:

    a. The examiner shows a picture and asks, "If an equal number of flowers is put in each vase, how many flowers will be in each?"

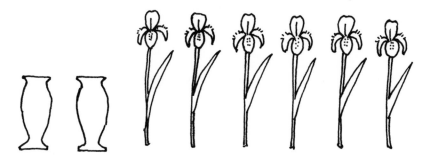

    b. Given a pencil and a sheet on which are printed problems such as these, the test-taker is asked to solve as many as he can.

$$4\overline{)8} \quad 6\overline{)18} \quad 5\overline{)145} \quad 17\overline{)20.4}$$

$$2/5 \div 1/4 = \underline{\hspace{1cm}} \qquad .55 \div 5\ 1/2 = \underline{\hspace{1cm}}$$

33. The test-taker is asked to work visually-presented arithmetic problems in his head. Problems such as the following are given:

    a. The test-taker is asked to tell what number goes in the box.

$$2 + 5 = \square \qquad 3 + \square = 4 \qquad \square + 3 = 9$$

    b. The test-taker is asked to tell what number goes in the circle, using the number from the first blank to fill in the second blank:

$$3 + 2 = \underline{\hspace{0.8cm}} \qquad 4 \times \underline{\hspace{0.8cm}} = 12 \qquad 7 \times 4 = \underline{\hspace{0.8cm}}$$

$$1 + \underline{\hspace{0.8cm}} = \bigcirc \qquad \underline{\hspace{0.8cm}} - 2 = \bigcirc \qquad \underline{\hspace{0.8cm}} + 6 = \bigcirc$$

34. The test-taker is asked to tell what additional information is needed to solve problems such as these:

The Walker family spends $30 more each week on groceries than the Green family. How much is the Walker family weekly grocery bill?

Bill, June, and Sarah entered a bicycle race. Bill finished the race in an hour and a half, June finished it in an hour and a quarter, and Sarah finished it in an hour and thirty-five minutes. What was their average speed?

35. The test-taker is asked to respond to items related to monetary value, such as these:

   a. Why would you expect the middle bottle to cost more than the others?

   b. The test-taker is shown money, coins and bills, or a facsimile of money and is asked to tell its value or to work problems involving money.

   c. The test-taker is asked to read a graph.

   d. The test-taker is asked to read a check drawn on a bank.

   e. The test-taker is asked to tell which of a variety of coins and bills should be given to the clerk to pay for an article of a certain price.

   f. The test-taker is asked to tell which of two different sizes of products is the better value, considering cost per unit of volume or weight.

   g. The test-taker is asked to indicate what coins and/or bills should be used in making change for a purchase of a given amount.

   h. The test-taker is asked to read and use information from check stubs and bank statements.

36. The test-taker is asked to identify by use and to "read" pictures of various measures, such as length, temperature, mass, and volume. Tasks such as the following are given:

   How much liquid is in this measuring cup?

37. The test-taker is asked to estimate a measure, such as height or weight, of an object by looking at a picture of it in which a scale indicator is also shown or is given in the oral presentation of the problem. Tasks such as the following are given:

If this car is 4½ feet high, about how tall is the lamp post?

If the carton of milk on the right weighs two pounds, about how much will the carton on the left weigh?

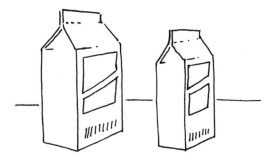

38. The test-taker is asked to demonstrate understanding of relationships of common measures by answering questions such as:

   One decimeter is how many centimeters?

   At about what room temperature do most people begin to feel chilly?

   One quart plus one cup is how many ounces?

   How would you feel about carrying a suitcase that weighs ninety pounds?

   One-half gross is how many things?

39. The test-taker is asked questions about large and small measures of time. Questions such as the following are asked:

   How many minutes are in ¾ of an hour?

   For what is a calendar used?

   What time does this clock show?

If today is the 22nd of May, in how many more days will it be the fourth of next month?

MAY			1	2	3	4
5	6	7	8	9	10	11
12	13	14	15	16	17	18
19	20	21	22	23	24	25
26	27	28	29	30		

40. The test-taker is asked to count a number of objects and then is asked to match that number with an equivalent number of other objects. Tasks such as the following are presented:

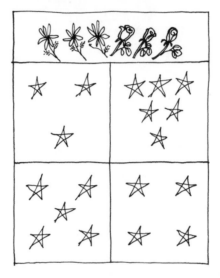

Look at these daisies and roses. Count how many there are altogether. How many stars does that equal? Point to the box that shows the same number of stars.

41. The test-taker is asked to count a number of objects and to match that number with the numeral that shows how many objects there are. Tasks such as the following are presented:

10	2
5	4

Count these cups. Point to the numeral that shows how many cups there are.

42. The test-taker is asked questions involving place value, such as:

Which of these numbers has the digit 4 in the hundreds place?

6834   5439   7846   4289

Which of these numbers represents nine thousands and three units?

30903	9030	9003	903

43. The test-taker is asked to demonstrate the ability to solve problems of area, volume, and perimeter, such as:

    If a garden is 6 meters by 10 meters, what is its area in square meters?

44. The test-taker is asked to demonstrate his understanding of numbers in problems such as:

    How many tens are there in a hundred?

    Which number is represented by this expression? $5(10)^3 + 2(10)^2 + 6$

5326	5260	5226	5206

45. The test-taker is asked to work with problems involving exponents, such as:

    Factor this expression. $X^2 - 2X - 15$

    Which term is represented by this ratio? $\dfrac{y^6}{y^3}$

$y^{3.6}$	y^3	y	y^6

46. The test-taker is asked to tell which of a number of expressions are not equal to a given number, such as:

    Which expression is not equal to 5 times 564?

    $(10 \times 564) \div 2$ $(5 \times 500) + (5 \times 64)$ $(5 \times 600) - 36$ $(5 \times 600) - 64$

47. The test-taker is asked to solve problems in geometry, such as:

    The diameter of a circle is ten inches. What is the approximate area of the circle?

    If the two sides adjoining the right angle of a right-angled triangle are 6 inches and 8 inches, what is the area of this triangle in square inches?

    If the earth makes one full rotation every 24 hours, through how many degrees will it have rotated in eight hours?

48. The test-taker is asked to solve problems involving two unknowns, such as the following:

    If $4X + 6Y = 0$ and $2X + Y = 4$, then what is the value of Y?
    In which equation would X rise in value when Y increases?

    $X + Y = 36$ $XY = 36$ $X = 36Y$ $X = \dfrac{36}{Y}$

49. The test-taker is asked to solve problems requiring him to work with decimals and percents, such as:

    Write as a decimal: $1/5 = $ _____

    30% of 120 = _____

    A city's current population is 1.03 times the size of its population last year. What percent is its present population of its former population?

50. The test-taker is asked to solve problems or identify formulas in solid geometry. Tasks such as, "Give the formula for finding the surface area of a right circular cone," are given.

51. The test-taker is asked to tell which one(s) of the equations, such as these, when graphed, would pass through the origin:

$$y = 2x = 3 \qquad y = x^2 \qquad 2y = x^3 \qquad y = x^2 + 4$$

52. The test-taker is asked to solve a problem such as:

    What is the value of 5 factorial?

53. The test-taker is asked to solve a problem such as:

    In the triangle shown, what is the cosine of A?

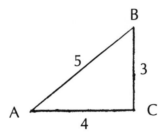

54. The test-taker is asked to solve algebra problems, such as:

    $x + 7 = 10$ if $x = 4$, $y = 5$;

    $x = $ ___ $x^3 (2y) = $ _____

55. The test-taker is asked to find the mean, median, or mode of a group of numbers, such as the following:

    7, 8, 23, 42, 34, 23, 25

56. The test-taker is asked to find the square root of a number such as 2041.

57. The test-taker is asked to solve problems in logarithms, such as: $\log_3 71$

READING

READING

Tasks such as the following are used to assess how well an individual can perform the various aspects of reading, such as using phonics, identifying words or letters, and comprehending what is read.

1. The test-taker is asked to identify letters of the alphabet, such as those shown below:

2. The test-taker is asked to read words aloud, such as:

          got   winter   extra   technical   fiduciary

3. The test-taker is asked to read a sentence to himself and then, without referring back to the sentence, choose from among a number of pictures the one that best shows the meaning of what he has read. Sentences and pictures such as the following are given:

    The cat came to the girl.

The pair in the tree was beautiful.

He rose from the chair with alacrity.

4. The test-taker is asked to pronounce nonsense syllables, such as the following:

    com   ano   und   blotap   semicolandorp   thalinsoph

5. The test-taker is asked to read and complete analogies, such as:

    month-week: hour-_____
    cattle-calves: goats-_____
    ecstatic-joyous: depressed-_____

6. The test-taker is instructed to read one or more sentences to himself and then tell the examiner a word to go in the blank space. Some of the items may have accompanying pictures that show the meaning of the passage. Sentences such as the following are given:

    The girl is riding a _____.

    Oil is used to keep machines running smoothly. The moving parts are lubricated with _____.

    Although many consider people holding public office in the United States to be of _____ character, most office holders are conscientious, patriotic, moral people.

REASONING

REASONING

The ability to solve problems is assessed using tasks such as these.

1. The individual being tested is asked such questions as:

   Do wheels turn?

   Do flowers talk?

   Do alligators shop?

   Do sailors navigate?

   Do philosophers contemplate?

2. The examiner asks the test-taker to tell what is not right or is foolish in statements such as these:

   Ellen used the bucket with no bottom in it to carry water from the well.

   My mother's wife is handsome, though he is bald.

   Because I am an only child, my brothers and sisters tease me.

   Jim played the title role in the class play, *The Tempest*.

3. The examiner asks the test-taker to solve practical problems requiring the use of common sense. The problems are similar to the following:

   What is the thing to do when you get a headache?

   What is the thing to do if the milk you are drinking, or the food you are eating, tastes spoiled?

   What is the thing to do if you are playing a game and the other person cheats you?

4. The examiner asks the test-taker about familiar events, customs, and attitudes, such as:

   What do we do with our noses?

   Why do people have cars or trucks?

   Why should people learn to read?

   Why is it important for the labels on food to list what is in the food?

   Why do we have to pay taxes on many of the things we buy?

   In what ways are large cars better than small cars?

   What are the advantages of having a president of the United States?

5. The test-taker is asked to respond to items such as these:

    Put your left hand above your right hand.

    Show me my left leg.

    If today is Thursday, what day was the day before yesterday?

    How can you figure which years are leap years?

6. The test-taker is asked to indicate how the parts of a puzzle go together to make a coherent whole, either by actually assembling them or by telling how they should be arranged. Puzzles such as the following are used:

7. The test-taker is asked to use a pencil to mark the path that should be taken through a maze. Mazes such as the following are used:

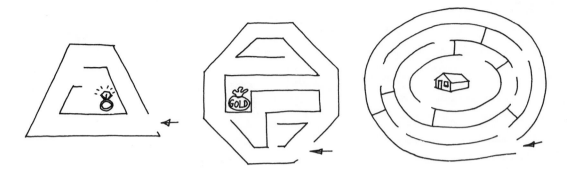

8. The test-taker folds a small piece of paper one or more times and then makes a cut through the folded paper. The test-taker is then given paper and pencil and asked to mark where the folds and cuts would be if the paper were unfolded.

9. The examiner presents sentences with an essential word, or words, missing and asks the test-taker to complete it. The task may be either written or oral. Sentences such as the following are presented:

    When we got to the lake we had a picnic _____ then went fishing.

    She is feeling much better _____ she got the medicine she needed.

    The space shuttle is expensive _____ not _____ expensive _____ building a new ship for each trip.

10. After giving the test-taker a pencil and a drawing of a rectangle with a break at one corner, the test-taker is asked to suppose that the rectangle represents a field that is going to be flooded when a new dam is closed. The tiny malodeuria flower, an endangered species, has been known to grow in that field. It is the test-taker's job to search the field to find all of them so they may be transplanted in safe ground. Letting the opening represent the gate, the test-taker is told to mark with a pencil how he would conduct the search. The examiner notes whether or not a logical and effective searching strategy is used.

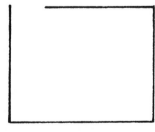

11. The examiner describes a situation to the test-taker and then asks him to name the event or explain what is happening. Descriptions and questions such as the following are given:

    Children were busily working in a classroom and a teacher was instructing a small group of them. Suddenly there was a loud noise. The children, followed by the teacher, got up immediately, left the room, and went outside. What was going on?

    A man got out of a car that had a red, white, and blue poster taped to each side. He then went to each house on the street, spoke enthusiastically to each person who came to the door, usually shook each person's hand, and always gave each person a small card. What do you think the man was doing?

12. The test-taker is given a card on which are printed scrambled sentences. He is then asked to unscramble the sentences. Sentences such as the following are presented:

quickly home he toward walked

man up chair old got his the slowly from

compete the of flag children the for honor the raising

13. The examiner presents (and may repeat) situations and questions such as the following:

John said that he phoned Mary but no one answered. Mary said that she was home until noon, and that Henry did not leave until an hour later. Mary returned at two in the afternoon. When must John have phoned?

14. The test-taker is asked to solve problems such as these:

Suppose you were facing east, which hand would be toward the south?

If you were going west, what direction would you be going if you turned to the left?

If you were facing south and walked two miles, then turned to the right and walked one mile, then turned to the right again and walked two miles, then turned to the left, in what direction would you be facing? How far would you be from your starting point?

15. The test-taker is shown a message in code and decoded. He is instructed to use this model as a key in coding another message. The key and the message to be coded are similar to the example shown below:

ECNN   E J C F   _____

CA L L   CHAD   TOMORROW

16. The individual being tested is asked to arrange pictures such as these to tell a logical story.

17. The test-taker is asked to arrange blocks that either copy designs made with other blocks by the examiner or that copy designs shown on cards. The blocks are identical and their opposite sides are identical, much like the ones illustrated below:

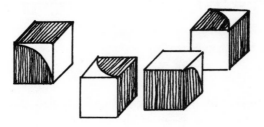

Designs to be copied are similar to these:

RECEPTIVE LANGUAGE

RECEPTIVE LANGUAGE

The ability to understand spoken language is assessed using tasks such as these:

1. The individual being tested is asked such questions as:

   Do wheels turn?

   Do flowers talk?

   Do alligators shop?

   Do sailors navigate?

   Do philosophers contemplate?

2. A page of designs set in rows is placed before the test-taker. The examiner then gives the test-taker a series of increasingly complex instructions as to how he is to mark the designs with a pencil. Designs such as the following are used:

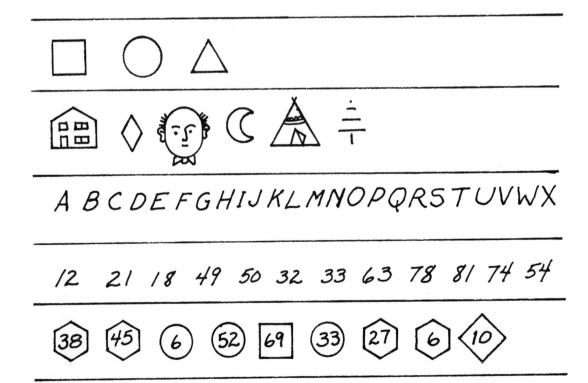

Marking begins after each set of oral instructions is given.. Instructions such as the following are given:

> Put a circle in the triangle and a line in the box.

> Put a ring around the moon, a line over the house, and a dot under the tree.

> Put circles around the number that is in the twenties, the number that is one less than 8 X 8, the number that is 6 X 2, the number that is 10 X 5, and the last number in line.

> Put circles under the 6 in a hexagon, the odd number in a circle, the biggest number in a hexagon, and the odd number in the hexagon nearest ten.

3. The examinee is asked to perform a task, or tasks, in a certain order. Tasks such as the following are given:

> Put this ruler on the desk.

> Put this eraser beside the tablet, move the chair up to the table, then bring me the ruler.

4. The examiner says a word and then asks the test-taker to indicate which of a number of pictures best illustrates that word. Words and pictures such as the following are used:

Examiner says, "Point to the clock."

Examiner says, "Point to the goose."

5. The test-taker is shown a picture of an animal, such as a dog, and asked to indicate major features of its anatomy as the examiner names them.

6. As the test-taker is shown miniature common objects such as a cup, bird, bowl, motorcycle, jar, and insect, the examiner asks him to name them.

7. Common objects, either pictured or miniaturized, are shown to the test-taker. The examiner then describes each by use and asks the test-taker to point to each one as it is described. Directions such as the following are given:

   Show me what we sleep on.

   Show me what we write with.

   Show me what we use to keep our teeth clean.

SPELLING

SPELLING

Tasks such as the following are used to indicate how well an individual can perform various aspects of spelling, such as discriminating letters from each other and from other shapes, and using phonics and memory of letter sequences to spell words.

1. The test-taker is asked to look at a group of designs and find the one that is a letter of the alphabet. Designs such as the following are used:

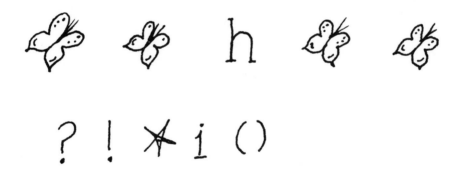

2. The examiner says a word, uses it in a sentence, and then asks the test-taker to select the sequence of letters on a printed card that spells the word. Items such as the following are given:

    Home. His *home* is next to mine.
    play   home   one   for

    Fighter. The tall *fighter* won the boxing match.
    fiter   feiter   fitter   fighter

    Aerie. The eagle's *aerie* was at the edge of the cliff.
    aerie   airy   eerie   hairy

3. The examiner says a word, uses it in a sentence, then asks the test-taker to either print, write, or spell the word aloud. Words such as the following are used:

    do   is   hurt   related   thermal   myopic   inchoate

VISUAL DISCRIMINATION

VISUAL DISCRIMINATION

Tasks such as the following are used to measure the individual's alertness to visual stimuli.

1. The examiner points to the center picture and asks, "What goes best with this?"

2. The examiner points to the top left picture in the grid of four and then to the bottom left picture and says, "If this goes with this, then which of these six pictures should go with this picture (pointing to the one next to the top left)?"

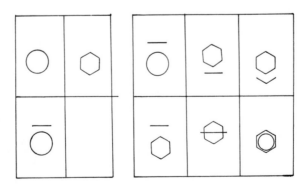

3. After drawing the test-taker's attention to the objects to be found in the drawing (mice in this example), the examiner asks him to see how many he can find in a limited time.

These are mice:

How many can you find in this picture?

4. The test-taker is shown three or more drawings, or designs, and asked to tell which one of the group does not belong.

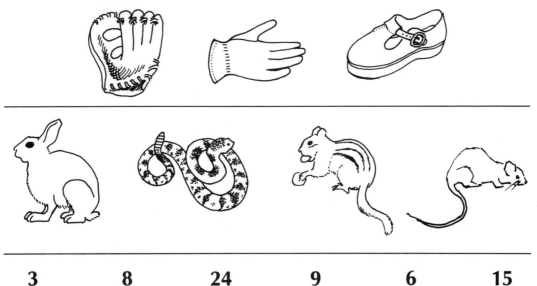

3   8   24   9   6   15

5. The test-taker is shown a picture and asked which of a number of other pictures shows the opposite of the first picture.

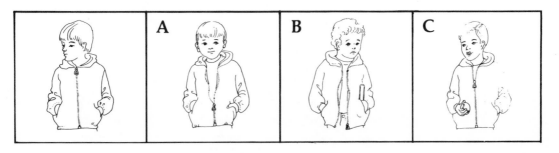

73

6. After placing a board with three removable disks on variously shaped pegs before the test-taker, the disks are removed while he watches. The test-taker is then asked to replace each disk on its appropriately shaped peg.

7. After placing a board with three removable disks on variously shaped pegs before the test-taker, the disks are removed while he watches. The board is then turned 180° and the test-taker is asked to return each disk to its appropriate peg.

8. After briefly showing the test-taker a drawing of one or more objects and making sure he knows the name(s) of the object(s), the examiner asks the test-taker to find the same drawing(s) on a page with a number of drawings done in a similar style. A drawing such as this is presented first:

The test-taker is then asked to find it on a page such as this.

9. The examiner shows the test-taker two or more items and asks him to compare them in a specific way. The examiner asks questions such as:

> Which is darker?

> Which is smallest?

> Which one is happiest?

10. After drawing the test-taker's attention to the model design, he is asked to find, on the same page, the identical design from among a number of similar or dissimilar designs. First, a drawing like this is presented:

Then the test-taker is asked to find it again in a group like this.

These are further examples of this type of task:

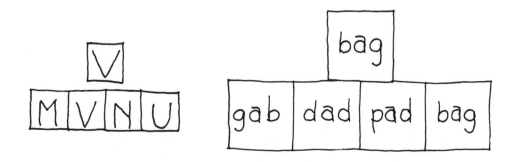

Visual Discrimination

11. The test-taker is given a quantity of objects, such as beads, and asked to sort them by a specific characteristic, such as size, color, or shape. This task may be timed.

12. The test-taker is shown a picture of objects, all of which are identical except one. The test-taker is asked to indicate the one object that is different. Pictures such as the following are used:

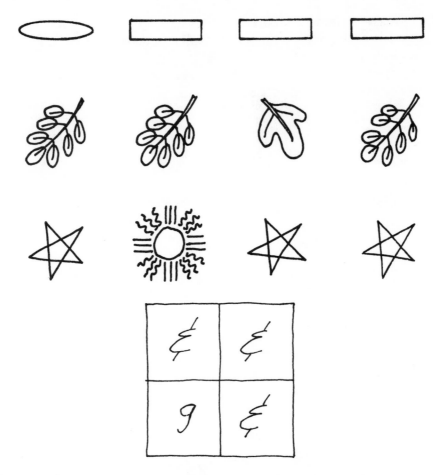

13. The test-taker is given a key and then asked to match designs and shapes as quickly as possible using that key. Keys and task formats similar to the following are used:

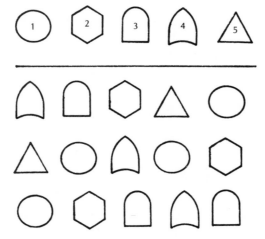

In this example the test taker is asked to place the correct number, from the key, in each of the shapes below the line.

14. The test-taker is shown a whole shape and then asked to choose from a number of other shapes the two (or more) that could be put together to form the whole shape. Shapes such as the following are used:

VISUAL MEMORY

VISUAL MEMORY

Tasks such as the following are used to assess an individual's ability to remember what he sees over either a long or short period of time.

1. The test-taker is shown a picture of an item. Then, from pictures of a variety of items, he is asked to find another one of the same kind. Pictures such as the following are used:

2. The examiner places a pile of tiles with various designs on the testing surface. Then, after putting just the tiles needed for the task before the test-taker, the examiner briefly displays a card showing the sequence into which the decorated tiles are to be placed. The test-taker is then given two chances to copy the sequence from memory. Design sequences such as the following are used:

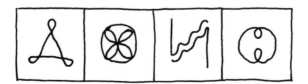

3. After drawing the test-taker's attention to the objects to be found in the drawing (mice in this example), the examiner asks him to see how many he can find in a limited time. Only a part of the object to be found is shown in the line drawing.

These are mice:

How many can you find in this picture?

4. After being shown a picture of an object, the test-taker is instructed to demonstrate (mime) appropriate actions for using it. Common items, such as a pencil, needle and thread, and bicycle, are pictured.

5. After briefly showing the test-taker a card with a sequence of pictures of common objects, the examiner asks him to list the objects from memory. The number of pictures on each card is very gradually increased. Cards showing pictures such as the following are used:

6. The test-taker is given part of a design. He is briefly shown the completed design and then asked to complete the design he was given from memory. Incomplete and complete designs such as these are used:

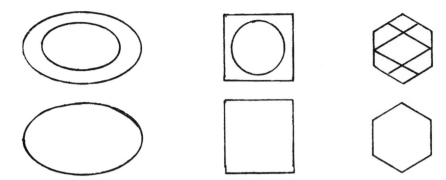

7. The test-taker is shown one, or more, designs briefly and then asked to draw the design or designs from memory. Designs such as the following are used:

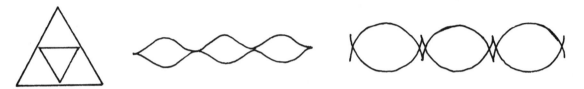

8. The test-taker is briefly shown cards with letters on them. He is then asked to list the letters from memory. The numbers of letters to be remembered is gradually increased. Letters such as these are presented:

    BH   GIF   NDQR   MLOZB

9. The examiner presents the test-taker with a picture that has been divided into equal pieces and the pieces scrambled. The test-taker is then asked to map how the parts of the picture should be placed to make a logical picture. The scrambled parts are numbered. These numbers are to be used to indicate on the "map" where each piece goes. The puzzles are similar to these:

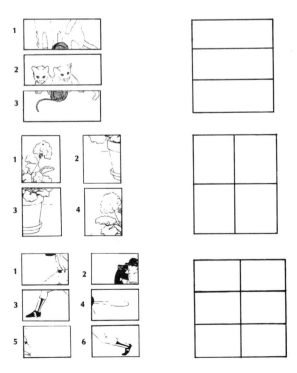

10. The examiner places three containers, with the open side down, before the test-taker. He is then shown a small toy and, while he watches, it is hidden under one of the containers. After a short delay, the test taker is asked to find the toy by lifting the appropriate container.

11. After briefly showing the test-taker a drawing of one or more objects and making sure he knows the name(s) of the object(s), the test-taker is asked to find the same drawing(s) on a page with a number of drawings done in a similar style. A drawing such as this is presented first:

The test-taker is then asked to find it on a page such as this.

12. A few small common objects are placed in a row before the test-taker. Each is named as it is placed before him. Then, while the objects are screened from the test-taker, one of them is removed. The test-taker is again shown the row of objects and is asked to tell which one is missing.

13. The test-taker is shown a partially finished line drawing of a common object. He is told what the drawing is of and is told one of the parts that is missing. Then he is given a pencil and asked to complete it. A drawing similar to this is given:

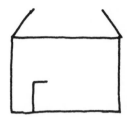

14. While the test-taker is watching, the examiner folds a piece of paper several times and then places the finished product flat against the table and holds it there. The test-taker is asked to fold an identical piece of paper in the same way.

15. While the test-taker is watching, the examiner ties a knot. The test-taker is then asked to make the same kind of knot in his piece of string.

16. The test-taker is asked to indicate what is missing in pictures similar to these:

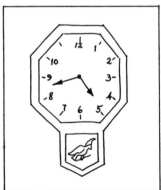 

17. While the test-taker is watching, the examiner strings beads of various kinds in a certain order and tells the test-taker he will be asked to string beads in the same order. After letting him look at the sequence for a short time, the model is put away and the test-taker is asked to duplicate it from memory. Sequences such as this are used:

VISUAL-MOTOR COORDINATION

Visual-Motor Coordination

Tasks such as the following are used to measure an individual's ability to coordinate his eye and hand movements.

1. The individual taking the test is asked to copy one or more geometric designs. He is given ample paper on which to make his drawings. Designs such as the following are used:

2. After being shown a picture of an object, the test-taker is instructed to demonstrate (mime) appropriate actions for using it. Common items, such as a pencil, needle and thread, and bicycle, are pictured.

3. After demonstrating how to do it, the examiner asks the test-taker to make a cross inside each shape as quickly as he can. Staying within the lines is stressed. The task is similar to putting a cross within shapes such as those shown below.

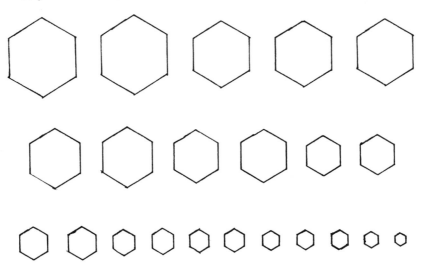

4. The test-taker is given part of a design. He is briefly shown the completed design and then asked to complete the design he was given from memory. Incomplete and complete designs such as these are used:

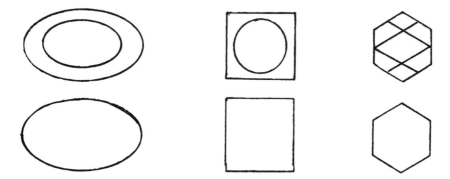

5 The test-taker is shown one or more designs briefly and then asked to draw the design or designs from memory. Designs such as these are used:

6. After placing a board with three removable disks on variously shaped pegs before the test-taker, the disks are removed while he watches. The test-taker is then asked to replace each disk on its appropriately shaped peg.

7. After placing a board with three removable disks on variously shaped pegs before the test-taker, the disks are removed while he watches. The board is then turned 180°, and the test-taker is asked to return each disk to its appropriate peg.

8. After building a tower a few blocks high, the examiner gives the test-taker a supply of blocks and asks him to build an identical tower.

9. The examiner demonstrates how objects, such as bobbins, beads, or spools, can be put on a string. He then gives the test-taker the necessary equipment and asks him to do the same.

10. The examiner demonstrates how a bridge can be built with blocks. The test-taker is then asked to copy the examiner's bridge using identical blocks.

11. The test-taker is asked to use a pencil to draw a very simple design, such as a dot or a "happy face."

12. The test-taker is asked to put the parts of a puzzle together to make a coherent whole. Puzzles such as the following are used:

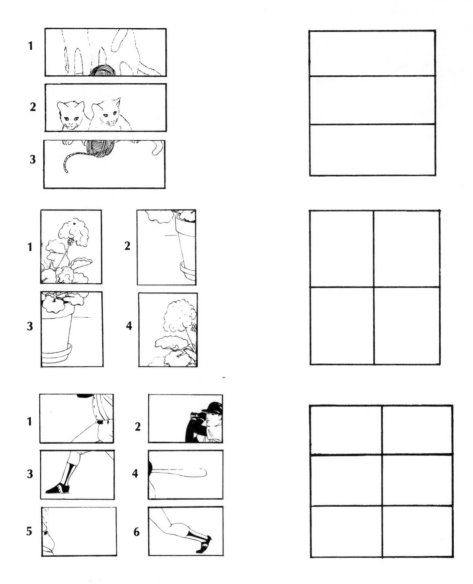

13. The test-taker is given a quantity of objects, such as beads, and asked to sort them by a specific characteristic, such as size, color, or shape.

14. The test-taker is shown a partially finished line drawing of a common object. He is told what the drawing is of and is told one of the parts that is missing. Then he is given a pencil and asked to complete it. A drawing similar to this is given:

.5. While the test-taker is watching, the examiner folds a piece of paper several times and then places the finished product flat against the table and holds it there. The test-taker is then asked to fold an identical piece of paper in the same way.

16. While the test-taker is watching, the examiner ties a knot. The test-taker is then asked to make the same kind of knot in his piece of string.

17. The test-taker is asked to use a pencil to mark the path that should be taken through a maze. Mazes such as the following are used:

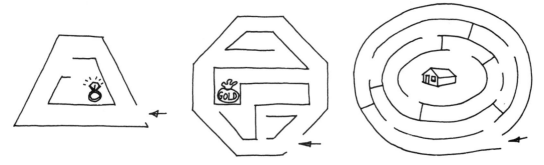

18. While the test-taker is watching, the examiner strings beads of various kinds in a certain order and tells the examinee he will be asked to string beads in the same order. After letting him look at the sequence for a short time, the model is put away and the test-taker is asked to duplicate it from memory. Sequences such as this are used:

19. The test-taker is asked to arrange blocks to either copy designs made with other blocks by the examiner or to copy designs shown on cards. The blocks are identical and their opposite sides are identical, much like the ones illustrated.

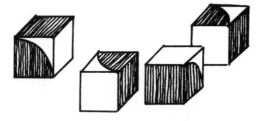

Designs to be copied are similar to these:

20. The test-taker is given a key and then asked to match designs and shapes as quickly as possible, using that key. Keys and task formats similar to the following are used:

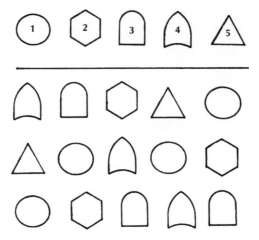

21. The test-taker is asked to copy, in a confined space, small letter-like designs as quickly as he can. Designs such as the following are used:

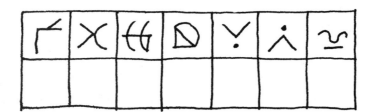

TEST–SUBTEST INDEX

Beery-Buktenica Developmental Test of Visual-Motor Integration, VMC 1

Bender Visual Motor Gestalt Test, VMC 1

Columbia Mental Maturity Scale, CT 5 (e), VD 4

Detroit Test of Learning Aptitude
 Pictorial Absurdities, EL 5, EI 2
 Verbal Absurdities, EL 6, R 2, EI 3
 Pictorial Opposites, CT 6, VD 5
 Verbal Opposites, EL 7, CT 7
 Motor Speed and Precision, VMC 3
 Auditory Attention Span for Unrelated Words, AM 5
 Oral Commissions, RL 3, AM 6
 Social Adjustment A, EL 8, R 3, EI 4
 Visual Attention Span for Objects, VM 5, C 5
 Orientation, R 5, CT 8, EI 6
 Free Association, EL 10
 Memory for Designs, VM 6, 7; VMC 1, 4, 5; C 6, 7
 Auditory Attention Span for Related Syllables, AM 7
 Number Ability, NR 1, 2, 3, 4, 5, 6
 Social Adjustment B, EL 9, R 4, EI 5
 Visual Attention Span for Letters, VM 8, C 9
 Disarranged Pictures, R 6, VM 9, C 10
 Oral Directions, RL 2, NR 7, AM 8, C 11
 Likenesses and Differences, EL 11, 12; CT 9, 10

Goldman-Fristoe-Woodcock Test of Auditory Discrimination
 Quiet Subtest, AD 1
 Noise Subtest, AD 2

Illinois Test of Psycholinguistic Abilities
 1. Auditory Reception, RL 1, R 1
 2. Visual Reception, CT 1, VM 1
 3. Visual Sequential Memory, VM 2, C 2
 4. Auditory Association, EL 1, CT 2

 5. Auditory Sequential Memory, AM 1, C 3
 6. Visual Association, CT 3, 4; VD 1, 2
 7. Visual Closure, VM 3, VD 3
 8. Verbal Expression, EL 2
 9. Grammatic Closure, EL 3
 10. Manual Expression, EI 1, VM 4, VMC 2
 11. Auditory Closure, EL 4, AM 3
 12. Sound Blending, AM 4

Key Math
 A. Numeration, EL 3 (c); NR 23, 24, 25, 20, 21, 22, 2, 5, 14
 B. Fractions, NR 26
 C. Geometry and Symbols, NR 27, 28
 D. Addition, NR 29
 E. Subtraction, NR 30
 F. Multiplication, NR 31
 G. Division, NR 32
 H. Mental Computation, NR 4 (a), C 16
 I. Numerical Reasoning, NR 33
 J. Word Problems, NR 4 (b)
 K. Missing Elements, NR 34
 L. Money, NR 35
 M. Measurements, NR 36, 37, 38
 N. Time, NR 39

Peabody Individual Achievement Test (PIAT)
 1. Mathematics, NR 1, 2, 3, 4 (b), 5, 12, 13, 14, 17, 20, 21, 26, 27, 29, 35 (b), 38, 39, 40, 42, 43, 44, 45, 46, 47, 48, 49, 50, 51, 52; VD 9, 10
 2. Reading Recognition, Rdg 1, 2; VD 10
 3. Reading Comprehension, Rdg 3
 4. Spelling, Rdg 1, 2; VD 12, S 1, 2
 5. Information, EL 25, EI 11

Peabody Picture Vocabulary Test (PPVT), RL 4

Stanford-Binet Intelligence Scale, Form L-M
 Age Level: II
 1. Three Hole Form Board, VD 6, VMC 6

Index

2. Delayed Response, VM 10
3. Identifying Parts of the Body, RL 5
4. Block Building: Tower, VMC 8
5. Picture Vocabulary, EL 13
6. Word Combinations, EL 14
A. Identifying Objects by Name, RL 6

Age Level: II-6
1. Identifying Objects by Use, RL 7
2. Identifying Parts of the Body, RL 5
3. Naming Objects, EL 15
4. Picture Vocabulary, EL 13
5. Repeating 2 Digits, AM 1, C 3
6. Obeying Simple Commands, RL 3, AM 6
A. Three-hole Form Board Rotated, VD 7, VMC 7

Age Level: III
1. Stringing Beads, VMC 9
2. Picture Vocabulary, EL 13
3. Block Building: Bridge, VMC 10
4. Picture Memories, VM 11, VD 8
5. Copying a Circle, VMC 11
6. Drawing a Vertical Line, VMC 11
A. Repeating 3 Digits, AM 1, C 3

Age Level: III-6
1. Comparison of Balls, NR 1, VD 9
2. Patience: Pictures, R 6, VMC 12
3. Discrimination of Animals, VD 10
4. Response to Pictures: Level I, EL 16, EI 7
5. Sorting Buttons, VD 11, VMC 13
6. Comprehension I, EL 9, R 4, EI 5
A. Comparison of Sticks, VD 9, NR 1

Age Level: IV
1. Picture Vocabulary, EL 13
2. Naming Objects from Memory, VM 12
3. Opposite Analogies I, CT 2
4. Pictorial Identification, RL 7
5. Discrimination of Forms, VD 10
6. Comprehension II, EL 9, R 4, EI 5
A. Memory for Sentences, AM 7, C 8

Age Level: IV-6
1. Aesthetic Comparison, VD 9
2. Opposite Analogies, EL 1, CT 2
3. Pictorial Similarities and Differences, VD 12
4. Materials, EL 17, EI 8
5. Three Commissions, AM 6, C 1
6. Comprehension III, EL 9, R 4, EI 5
A. Pictorial Identification, RL 7

Age Level: V
1. Picture Completion: Man, VM 13, VMC 14
2. Paper Folding: Triangle, VM 14, VMC 15
3. Definitions, EL 18
4. Copying a Square, VMC 1
5. Pictorial Similarities and Differences, VD 12
6. Patience: Rectangles, R 6, VMC, 12
A. Knot, VM 15, VMC 16

Age Level: VI
1. Vocabulary, EL 18
2. Differences, EL 12, CT 10
3. Mutilated Pictures, VM 16
4. Number Concepts, NR 8

5. Opposite Analogies, EL 1, CT 2
6. Maze Tracing, R 7, VMC 17
A. Response to Pictures: Level II, EL 16, EI 7

Age Level: VII
1. Picture Absurdities I, EL 5, EI 2
2. Similarities: Two Things, EL 11, CT 9
3. Copying a Diamond, VMC 1
4. Comprehension IV, EL 9, R 4, EI 5
5. Opposite Analogies III, EL 1, CT 2
6. Repeating 5 Digits, AM 1, C 3
A. Repeating 3 Digits Reversed, AM 3, C 4

Age Level: VIII
1. Vocabulary, EL 18
2. Memory for Stories: The Wet Fall, AM 9, C 12
3. Verbal Absurdities I, EL 6, R 2, EI 3
4. Similarities and Differences, EL 11, 12; CT 9
5. Comprehension IV, EL 8, 9; R 3, 4; EI 4, 5
6. Naming the Days of the Week, EI 9
A. Problem Situations I, R 11, EI 10

Age Level: IX
1. Paper Cutting, R 8
2. Verbal Absurdities II, EL 6, R 2, EI 3
3. Memory for Designs I, VM 7, VMC 5, C 7
4. Rhymes: New Form, EL 19
5. Making Change, NR 4
6. Repeating 4 Digits Reversed, AM 2, C 4
A. Rhymes: Old Form, EL 19

Age Level: X
1. Vocabulary, EL 18
2. Block Counting, NR 9
3. Abstract Words I, EL 18 (l-r)
4. Finding Reasons, EL 9, R 4, EI 5
5. Word Naming, EL 10
6. Repeating 6 Digits, AM 1
A. Verbal Absurdities III, EL 6, R 2, EI 3

Age Level: XI
1. Memory for Designs I, VM 7, VMC 5, C 7
2. Verbal Absurdities IV, EL 6, R 2, EI 3
3. Abstract Words II, EL 18 (l-r)
4. Memory for Sentences II, AM 7, C 8
5. Problem Situations II, R 11, EI 10
6. Similarities: Three Things, EL 20, CT 11
A. Finding Reasons II, EL 9, R 4

Age Level: XII
1. Vocabulary, EL 18
2. Verbal Absurdities II, EL 6, EI 2
3. Picture Absurdities II, EL 5, EI 2
4. Repeating 5 Digits Reversed, AM 2, C 4
5. Abstract Words I, EL 18 (l-r)
6. Minkus Completion I, EL 21, R 9
A. Memory for Designs II, VM 7, VMC 5, C 7

Age Level: XIII
1. Plan of Search, R 10

2. Abstract Words II, EL 18 (l-r)
3. Memory for Sentences III, AM 7, C 8
4. Problems of Fact, R 11, EI 10
5. Dissected Sentences, EL 22, R 12
6. Copying a Bead Chain from Memory, VM 17, VMC 18, C 13
A. Paper Cutting, R 8

Age Level: XIV
1. Vocabulary, EL 18
2. Induction, NR 10
3. Reasoning, R 13
4. Ingenuity I, NR 11
5. Orientation: Direction I, R 14
6. Reconciliation of Opposites, EL 11 (g-j), CT 9 (g-j)
A. Ingenuity II, NR 11

Age Level: AA
1. Vocabulary, EL 18
2. Ingenuity I, NR 11
3. Differences Between Abstract Words, EL 12 (k-m), CT 10 (k-m)
4. Arithmetical Reasoning,, NR 12
5. Proverbs I, EL 23, CT 12
6. Orientation: Direction II, R 14
7. Essential Differences, EL 12 (j-m), CT 10 (j-m)
8. Abstract Words III, EL 18 (l-r)
A. Binet Paper Cutting, R 8

Age Level: SAI
1. Vocabulary, EL 18
2. Enclosed Box Problem, NR 13
3. Minkus Completion II, EL 21, R 9
4. Repeating 6 Digits Reversed, AM 2, C 4
5. Sentence Building, EL 24
6. Essential Similarities, EL 11, CT 9
A. Reconciliation of Opposites, EL 11 (g-j), CT 9 (g-j)

Age Level: SAII
1. Vocabulary, EL 18
2. Finding Reasons III, EL 9, EI 5
3. Proverbs II, EL 23, CT 12
4. Ingenuity I, NR 11
5. Essential Differences, EL 12 (j-m), CT 10 (j-m)
6. Repeating Thought of Passage I: Value of Life, AM 10, C 14
A. Codes, R 15

Age Level: SAIII
1. Vocabulary, EL 18
2. Proverbs III, EL 23, CT 12
3. Opposite Analogies V, EL 1, CT 2
4. Orientation: Direction III, R 8
5. Reasoning II, NR 13
6. Repeating Thought of Passage II: Tests, AM 10; C 14

A. Opposite Analogies V, EL 1, CT 2

Wechsler Scales: Wechsler Adult Intelligence Scale-Revised (WAIS-R); Wechsler Intelligence Scale for Children-Revised (WISC-R); Wechsler Preschool and Primary Scale of Intelligence (WPPSI)
Information, EL 25, EI 11
Similarities, EL 11, CT 9
Arithmetic, NR 2,4 (b), 12 and NR 1 for the WPPSI
Vocabulary, EL 18
Comprehension, EL 8, 9; R 3, 4; EI 4, 5
Picture Completion, VM 16
Block Design, R 17, VMC 19
WAIS-R, WISC-R Digit Span, AM 1, 2; C 3, 4
WPSSI Sentences, AM 7, C 8
WAIS-R, WISC-R Picture Arrangement, R 16, EI 12
WAIS-R, WISC-R Object Assembly, R 6, VMC 12
WAIS-R Digit Symbol, VD 13, VMC 20, C 15
WISC-R Coding, VD 13, VMC 20, C 15
WPPSI Animal House, VD 13, VMC 20, C 15
WISC-R, WPPSI Mazes, R 7, VMC 17
WPPSI Geometric Designs, VMC 11
Wepman Auditory Discrimination Test, AD 3
Wepman Auditory Discrimination Test-Revised, AD 4
Wide Range Achievement Test (WRAT)
Reading, Rdg 1, 2; VD 10
Spelling, VMC 21, S 3
Arithmetic NR 2, 4 (b), 5, 6, 8, 20, 22, 24 29 (b), 30 (b), 31, 32 (b), 39, 45 (a), 48, 49, 53, 54, 55, 56, 57
Woodcock Reading Mastery Tests
Letter Identification, Rdg 1
Word Identification, Rdg 2
Word Attack, Rdg 4
Word Comprehension, Rdg 5, CT 14
Passage Comprehension, Rdg 6

THE AUTHOR

Patricia W. Clemens, MA, is currently a school psychologist serving seven schools in the Grundy County School System, Tennessee. Prior to this work, she served as a licensed psychological examiner for the Franklin County School System, also in Tennessee.

Mrs. Clemens is a member of the National Association of School Psychologists, Tennessee Association of School Psychologists, and Council for Exceptional Children.